Jupiter

Jupiter

Elaine Landau

Watts LIBRARY

Franklin Watts
A Division of Grolier Publishing
New York • London • Hong Kong • Sydney
Danbury, Connecticut

For Michael
Your makeup—like Jupiter's—is that of a star.

Note to readers: Definitions for words in **bold** can be found in the Glossary at the back of this book.

Photographs ©: AKG London: 40 (Painting by Valentin Alexandrovich Serov), 6; Ancient Art & Architecture Collection Ltd.: 26; Art Resource, NY: 24 (Nimatallah); Bridgeman Art Library International Ltd., London/New York: 27 (Scenographia: Systematis Copernicani Astrological Chart, c. 1543, British Library); Corbis-Bettmann: 2 (Jay Pasachoff); Finley Holiday Films: 37 (NASA), cover, 5, 16, 20, 21, 29, 35, 44, 45; NASA: 8, 22, 46, 48; Photo Researchers: 18 (NASA/Science Source), 14 (NRAO/AUI/SPL), 31 (NASA/SPL); Photri: 12, 28, 32, 38, 41, 43; Tom Stack & Associates: 50 (NASA/JPL/Tsado); University of California, Lick Observatory: 52.

Solar system diagram created by Greg Harris

Visit Franklin Watts on the Internet at:
http://publishing.grolier.com

Library of Congress Cataloging-in-Publication Data

Landau, Elaine.
  Jupiter / by Elaine Landau
    p.   cm.— (Watts Library)
  Includes bibliographical references and index.
  Summary: Describes the characteristics of the planet Jupiter and its moons, as revealed by photographs sent back by unmanned spacecraft.
    ISBN 0-531-20387-5 (lib. bdg.)   0-531-16426-8 (pbk.)
    1. Jupiter (Planet)—Juvenile literature. [1. Jupiter (Planet)] I. Title. II. Series.
QB661.L36 1999
523.45—dc21   98-9917
                                                                  CIP
                                                                   AC

Contents

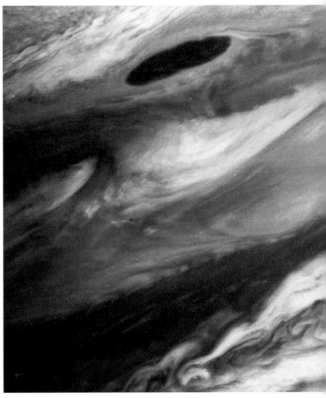

A marble sculpture of Jupiter—king of the Roman gods

Chapter One

King of the Planets

For much of the year, the planet Jupiter is the fourth brightest object in the sky. Humans first noticed Jupiter thousands of years ago, and have have watched it move across the night sky ever since.

The ancient Romans named the planet after the king of their gods. According to Roman legends, Jupiter—who was also called Jove—was the ruler of the Universe. The ancient symbol for the planet Jupiter is a lightning bolt. It represents the size and strength of the mighty

This color-enhanced view of Jupiter was created by combining a number of images taken by Voyager 1.

god after whom the planet was named. Although the stargazers of ancient Rome didn't know it, they'd picked the perfect name for the planet.

Jupiter really is the king of the planets. It is 88,846 miles (142,984 kilometers) across, making it the largest planet in the **solar system**. The solar system consists of the Sun and the nine planets, dozens of moons, **asteroids**, and **comets** that **orbit**, or move around, the Sun. As you can see in the illustration on pages 10 and 11, Jupiter is the fifth planet from the Sun.

Jupiter's Journey

Like Earth and all the other planets in the solar system, Jupiter orbits the Sun. Earth orbits the Sun in 365 days. Jupiter is much farther from the Sun than Earth, so the king of the planets takes much longer to complete a single orbit. Jupiter's long journey around the Sun requires more than 4,000 Earth-days. That's close to 12 Earth-years! Because a year is defined as the amount of time it takes for a planet to revolve around the Sun once, a year on Jupiter is about twelve times longer than a year on Earth.

All the objects in our solar system revolve around the Sun because they are trapped by a powerful but invisible force called **gravity**. The Sun's gravity pulls all the planets and other objects in the solar system toward the Sun. In the same way, Earth's gravity pulls the Moon and objects on our planet toward the center of Earth.

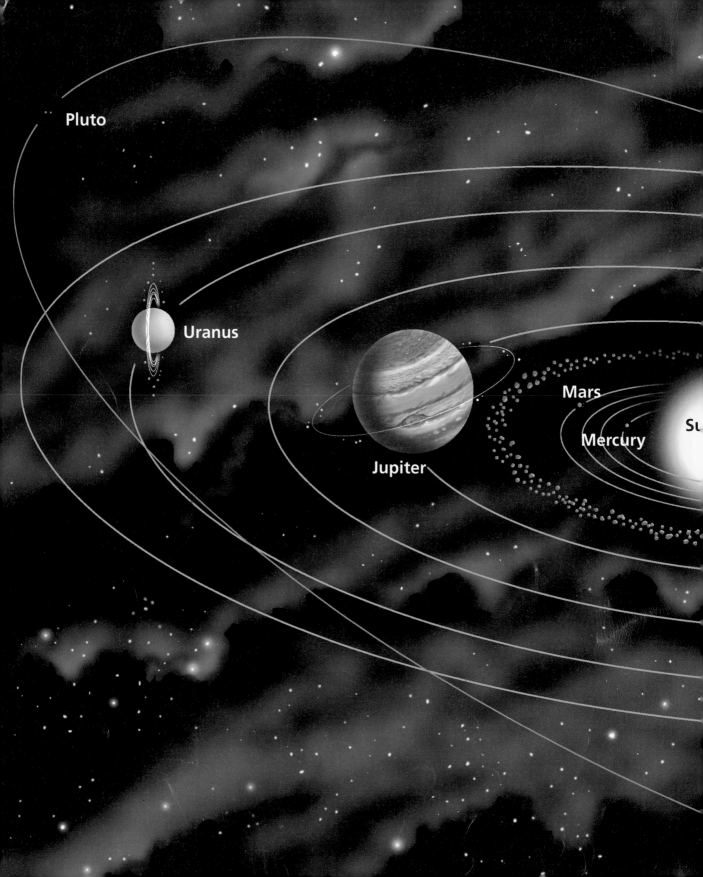

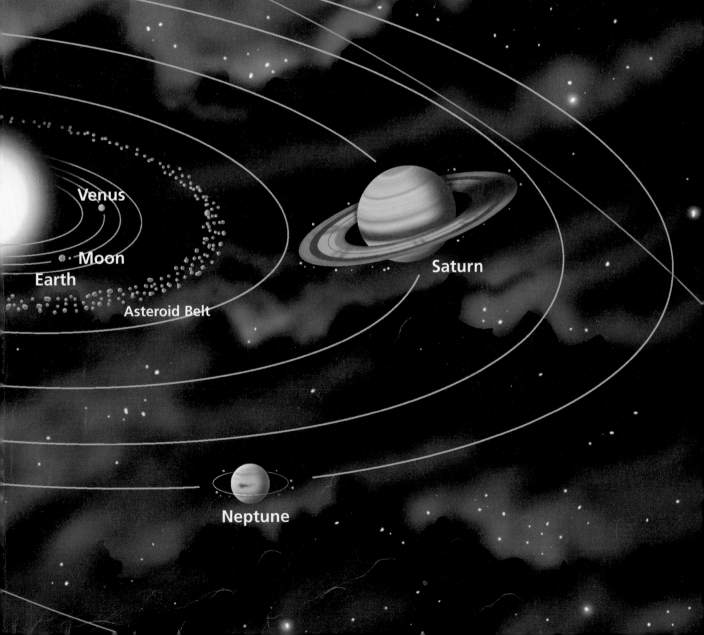

The Solar System

Venus

Moon

Earth

Asteroid Belt

Saturn

Neptune

Jupiter's gravity keeps its moons orbiting the planet. Io, one of Jupiter's many moons, is visible in this color-enhanced view of the king of the planets.

The force of gravity operates all around us. For example, if you toss a coin into the air, it will fall to the floor because gravity pulls the coin down. A kite will stay in the air as long as the wind is blowing, but when the wind stops, gravity pulls the kite to the ground.

Earth isn't the only planet with gravity. Jupiter has its own gravitational pull. Because Jupiter is much larger than Earth, its gravity is much stronger. The gravitational pull on Jupiter is two and a half times greater than the pull of gravity on Earth. In fact, no planet in the solar system has a stronger gravitational pull than Jupiter. The area over which a planet's gravity extends is called its **gravitational field**. Jupiter has a very strong gravitational field.

As Jupiter orbits the Sun, it also rotates, or turns, on its **axis**—an imaginary line through the center of a planet. Like Jupiter, the other planets rotate on an axis as they orbit the Sun. But no planet spins more rapidly than Jupiter. Earth rotates once every 23 hours and 56 minutes. Despite its tremendous size, Jupiter rotates once every 9 hours and 50 minutes. That means a day on Jupiter is much shorter than a day on Earth.

Jupiter's Magnetic Field

Besides a gravitational field, many planets have a **magnetic field**. A planet's magnetic field is similar to the magnetic field around the magnets you stick onto your refrigerator. If you hold a magnet close to your refrigerator, you can feel the pull,

A Speedy Spinner

Jupiter rotates so fast that the motion causes the planet to bulge at its center and flatten at its poles.

or attraction, between the two. If you hold the magnet a little farther away, you will not feel the same pull because the refrigerator is outside the magnet's magnetic field.

Of course, the magnetic field of a planet is much larger than the magnetic field of a refrigerator magnet. Jupiter's magnetic field stretches for millions of miles. Earth has a magnetic field, too, but it is about fourteen times weaker than Jupiter's.

Jupiter's magnetic field is so powerful that it traps **solar wind**—a stream of tiny particles that escape from the Sun and are hurled through space. These particles form **radiation belts** around Jupiter. Radio telescopes on Earth can detect the radiation given off by Jupiter's radiation belts.

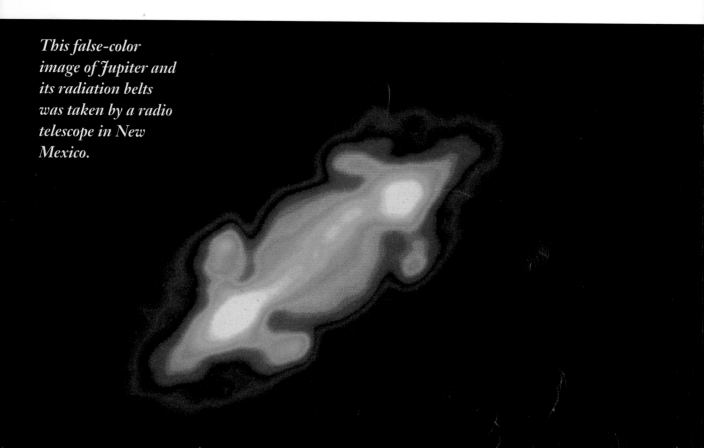

This false-color image of Jupiter and its radiation belts was taken by a radio telescope in New Mexico.

How Jupiter Measures Up

It may be difficult to imagine a planet as large as Jupiter. It is more than eleven times wider than Earth. If Jupiter were a hollow ball, more than 1,000 planets the size of Earth could easily fit inside it. If you combined all the other planets in the solar system into one great big ball, that ball would still be smaller than Jupiter.

Because Jupiter is larger than any other planet in the solar system, it also has the most **mass**. In other words, it contains more material than any other planet. In fact, Jupiter contains two-thirds of all the planetary mass in our entire solar system. Jupiter's mass is about 318 times greater than Earth's.

Mass is not the only measurement that scientists use to compare planets. They also look at **density**. Density describes the relationship between mass—the total amount of material in an object—and **volume**—the total amount of space the object

Almost a Star

In many ways, Jupiter is like a small sun, and the rings and moons that orbit Jupiter are like a miniature solar system. Like a sun, Jupiter is made mostly of hydrogen and helium. But Jupiter does not burn like a sun because it is too small. Our Sun is almost ten times larger than Jupiter and has more than 1,000 times more mass.

Because Jupiter is so much smaller than the Sun, it's **core** is too cool to burn. This may seem unbelievable when you learn that Jupiter's core can reach temperatures as high as 54,000 degrees Fahrenheit (30,000 degrees Celsius). Scientists believe that the temperature at the center of the Sun may be as reach 27,000,000°F (15,000,000°C). That's hot!

Jupiter is millions of miles away from Earth, but scientists can use computers to create an image that allows us to compare the sizes of the two planets. Earth is much smaller than Jupiter, but it is about four times denser than the king of the planets.

occupies. To find an object's density, you can divide its mass by its volume.

Imagine one measuring cup full of marshmallows and a second measuring cup full of pennies. Which is denser? Think about it. Marshmallows are light and fluffy. Pennies are smaller and fairly heavy. When the volume of pennies and marshmallows is equal, the mass of the pennies is much greater. This means that the density of the pennies is also much greater.

The planet Jupiter has more mass than all the other planets combined, so you might expect it to be the densest planet in the solar system. But don't forget, Jupiter is also much larger than the rest of the planets. In other words, it has a much greater volume than the other planets.

If you were to divide Jupiter's mass by its volume, you'd find out that Jupiter is not the densest planet in the solar system. In fact, Earth, Mercury, Venus, and Mars are all denser. Earth—the densest planet in the solar system—is about four times denser than Jupiter.

In this view of Earth from space, the brown area is Africa and the Middle East, the blue areas are ocean, and the white area at the bottom is Antarctica. The other white areas are the clouds in Earth's atmosphere.

Chapter Two

A Gas Giant

When you look at a photograph of Earth taken from space, you see the white swirling clouds in our **atmosphere**. Below the clouds, you can see the bright blue oceans and greenish-brown land that make up our planet's surface.

When you look at an image of Jupiter, you see the tops of the clouds high in its atmosphere, but you cannot see a solid surface below them. That's because Jupiter is not a solid planet the way Earth is. Jupiter is a gas giant—a huge ball of gases and liquids. Saturn, Neptune, and Uranus are gas giants too.

Colorful Clouds

If you look at Jupiter through a telescope, you can see the colorful clouds that make up its outer atmosphere. The clouds at the very top of the atmosphere are orange and red. The next layer of atmosphere has blue and white clouds. The lowest clouds are brown and orange. Sometimes it is possible to see the lower layers of clouds through holes in the upper layers. Scientists think that clouds at different levels have different colors because they are made of different materials. For exam-

This color-enhanced view of Jupiter's atmosphere is made up of many separate images that were combined by a computer. The computer fit the images together in the same way that we put together a jigsaw puzzle.

ple, the brown and orange clouds in the lowest layer may contain the chemicals sulfur and phosphorus.

Jupiter's clouds are in constant motion. Forceful winds push the clouds into their ever-changing patterns. Information collected by spacecraft that have flown by, orbited, and traveled into the upper layers of Jupiter's atmosphere show that the planet's winds blow as rapidly as 400 miles (645 km) per hour. During the worst hurricanes on Earth, wind speeds rarely exceed 150 miles (240 km) per hour.

Jupiter's winds blow in distinct bands. The light-colored bands are called **zones**, while the dark ones are known as **belts**. Some researchers suspect the light zones contain warmer gases that are rising, while the dark belts contain cooler gases that are sinking.

Sometimes small, white spots can be seen within the dark belts. Scientists believe that these oval-shaped spots, which are sometimes larger than the entire Earth, are severe storms similar to the hurricanes that occur on Earth. While hurricanes usually last only a few days, the storms on Jupiter may rage out of control for decades.

The light and dark colored bands in Jupiter's atmosphere are clearly shown in this color-enhanced view of the planet. Notice Jupiter's moon Io on the far right and the shadow of Ganymede on the far left.

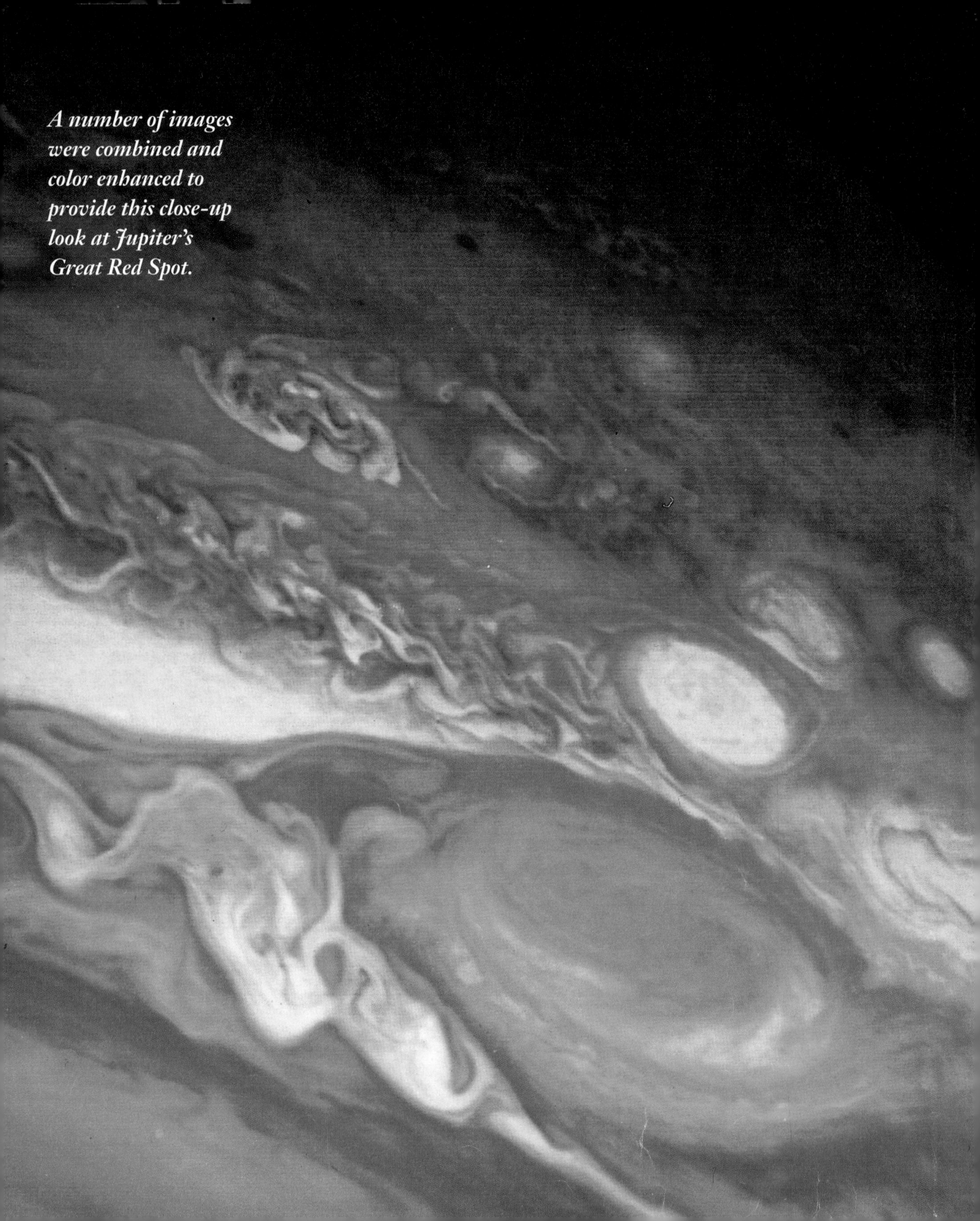

A number of images were combined and color enhanced to provide this close-up look at Jupiter's Great Red Spot.

One of the best-known storm centers on Jupiter is called the Great Red Spot. This giant, oval-shaped storm was first noticed by scientists more than 300 years ago. It is large enough to hold two Earths and whirls at a speed of 250 miles (400 km) per hour.

Below the Clouds

Jupiter's massive atmosphere puts a great deal of pressure on the materials deep within the planet. Because the pressure inside Jupiter is so much greater than the pressure on Earth, scientists suspect that the hydrogen layers inside the planet act very differently from hydrogen on Earth.

On our planet, hydrogen is a gas under normal conditions. But scientists believe that some of the hydrogen within Jupiter may form a layer of liquid metallic hydrogen. Below that layer is the planet's core. Some scientists think that Jupiter has a very small, rocky core deep inside, but other researchers disagree. They think the core is a liquid or a slushy mixture of solid and liquid materials. As you learned earlier, Jupiter's core is very hot. Because heat naturally flows from warmer areas to cooler areas, Jupiter's core is slowly releasing its heat.

As all that heat spreads outward through the planet's layers, it creates the strong winds that cause Jupiter's weather patterns. The weather patterns on Earth are influenced by the heat we receive from the Sun. While Earth gets most of its heat and light energy from the Sun, Jupiter gives off about twice as much energy as it receives from the Sun.

The Italian scientist Galileo Galilei discovered four of Jupiter's moons.

Chapter Three

From Galileo to *Galileo*

In 1609, an Italian scientist named Galileo Galilei learned of a new device being constructed in Holland—the telescope. Dutch sailors were using telescopes to search for land and spot other ships. Galileo quickly realized that telescopes could also be used to view the night sky. He learned how to build them, and constructed one for himself.

A year later, he was using his telescope to view the Moon and other objects in the the night sky. It wasn't long before he

Galileo made this telescope to study the nighttime sky.

noticed three little specks of light in line with the planet Jupiter. A few days later he observed a fourth speck of light. At first, he thought the objects were stars, but as he tracked their movement, he realized that they were orbiting Jupiter. Galileo knew those little specks of light must be moons. Because Galileo discovered these four moons, Io, Europa, Ganymede, and Callisto are often called the Galilean moons.

Spacecraft Visit Jupiter

It was almost 300 years before scientists began to make important new discoveries about Jupiter. By the late 1800s, telescopes had improved enough that it was possible to identify a fifth moon around Jupiter. During the first half of the twentieth century, scientists noticed seven more moons orbiting the king of the planets.

Despite these discoveries, most of the information we have about Jupiter has become available in the last few decades. It has been collected by **space probes**.

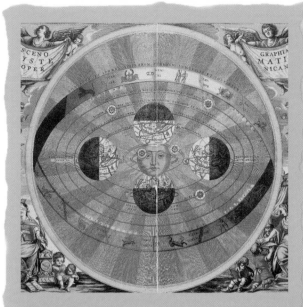

An Important Discovery

In the 1600s, most Europeans believed that Earth was at the center of the Universe and that the Sun and all the planets move around it. Galileo's discovery made him realize that a theory proposed about 70 years earlier by a Polish scientist named Nicolaus Copernicus was correct.

Copernicus had claimed that the Sun—not Earth—is at the center of our solar system. The illustration above shows how Copernicus envisioned the Universe.

Galileo reasoned that the planets must move around the Sun in the same way that Jupiter's moons move around Jupiter.

At first, very few people agreed with Galileo's idea. They refused to believe that the planets revolve around the Sun. As time passed, other scientists began to realize that Galileo—and Copernicus—had been right.

An artist's representation of Pioneer 11 *gathering information about the Great Red Spot*

In 1973, *Pioneer 10*, an unmanned space probe, flew within 81,000 miles (130,000 km) of Jupiter's cloud tops and sent more than 500 photographs back to Earth. No human-made object had ever come so close to the king of the planets. *Pioneer 10* also measured the amount of helium and hydrogen in Jupiter's atmosphere and made important discoveries about the planet's magnetic field and radiation belts.

In 1974, *Pioneer 11*, another unmanned space probe built and operated by the National Space and Aeronautic Administaration (NASA), flew even closer to Jupiter. It passed within 26,703 miles (43,000 km) of the planet, and took close-up photographs of Jupiter's polar regions. *Pioneer 11* also recorded information about the Great Red Spot and measured the temperature in several spots within Jupiter's atmosphere.

Voyager 1 and *Voyager 2*

In March 1979, the *Voyager 1* spacecraft provided scientists with even more information about the king of the planets. Most importantly, it detected a thin ring around the planet. A few months later, *Voyager 2* flew past Jupiter. It transmitted close-up photos of Jupiter's four largest moons back to Earth.

Voyager 1 provided NASA scientists with valuable information about Jupiter.

Where Are the Voyagers Now?

In all, the Voyager probes took more than 33,000 pictures of Jupiter and its moons. They then continued on their journey into space. Both probes provided photos of and information about Saturn in the early 1980s. In 1985 and 1986, *Voyager 2* flew past Uranus, discovering ten moons and at least eleven rings. In 1989, the probe flew past Neptune and sent images of that planet's rings back to Earth.

By February 1998, *Voyager 1* was more than 6.5 billion miles (10.5 billion km) from Earth. Both probes are now studying the environment of space in the outer solar system. They have enough fuel to operate until 2020.

Ulysses

In October 1990, the *Ulysses* space probe was launched by NASA and the European Space Agency (ESA)—a group of space scientists funded by several Western European nations. Although the probe's main purpose was to study the Sun's polar regions, it passed within 279,450 miles (450,000 km) of Jupiter in 1992.

Scientists took advantage of this opportunity to measure Jupiter's **magnetosphere**—the region of space affected by the planet's magnetic field. *Ulysses* also studied how solar wind and the radiation belts it forms around Jupiter affect the planet's magnetosphere.

Galileo

Some of our most exciting information about Jupiter has come from the *Galileo* spacecraft, which was named after Galileo Galilei. The probe was launched by NASA in October 1989. During the first 3 years of its journey, *Galileo* traveled within the inner solar system. It used the gravity of both Venus and Earth to build up enough speed to travel all the way to Jupiter. In 1995, Galileo finally reached Jupiter and began to orbit the huge planet.

During the next 2 years, *Galileo* orbited Jupiter eleven times and studied

Everyday Benefits

Equipment designed for the space program is sometimes adapted to improve things we use every day. Thanks to technology developed for the Galileo mission, our video cameras produce sharper images and our computers' memories are more efficient. In addition, radiation-resistant parts developed for *Galileo* are now used by some businesses and the military.

the planet's atmosphere and moons. *Galileo* also dropped a smaller probe 120 miles (190 km) into Jupiter's cloudy atmosphere. The probe had been designed to relay information for 75 minutes, but after 57 minutes, the tremendous heat and pressure of Jupiter's atmosphere disrupted the probe's communication system. Nevertheless, the probe gave scientists their first direct information about the mighty planet's fascinating atmosphere.

The Galileo mission cost about $1.3 billion to develop, build, and operate. That means that every U.S. citizen contributed 27 cents a year to pay for the 20-year effort.

An artist's idea of how Galileo *might have looked as its atmospheric probe was released*

This color-enhanced view of Jupiter and its four Galilean moons is a collage of images taken by Voyager 1. It was created by NASA scientists using a computer. The moons are not shown to scale, but they are in their proper positions relative to the planet.

Chapter Four

Jupiter's Moons and Rings

Scientists have now identified sixteen moons orbiting Jupiter. Some researchers think there may be more. The four moons closest to Jupiter are small, but the next four—the Galilean moons— are huge. The eight remaining moons are small and farther from Jupiter than the Galilean moons. Sinope, the moon farthest from Jupiter, is almost 15

Jupiter's Moons

Name	Distance from Jupiter		Distance Across		Year of Discovery
Metis	79,540 miles	(128,000 km)	25 miles	(40 km)	1979
Adrastea	80,160 miles	(129,000 km)	22 miles	(35 km)	1979
Amalthea	112,590 miles	(181,200 km)	106 miles	(170 km)	1892
Thebe	137,950 miles	(222,000 km)	47 miles	(75 km)	1979
Io	262,200 miles	(422,000 km)	2,257 miles	(3,632 km)	1610
Europa	416,900 miles	(671,000 km)	1,942 miles	(3,126 km)	1610
Ganymede	664,900 miles	(1,070,000 km)	3,278 miles	(5,276 km)	1610
Callisto	1,170,000 miles	(1,883,000 km)	2,995 miles	(4,820 km)	1610
Leda	6,891,000 miles	(11,090,000 km)	9 miles	(15 km)	1974
Himalia	7,120,900 miles	(11,460,000 km)	106 miles	(170 km)	1904
Lysithea	7,294,900 miles	(11,740,000 km)	22 miles	(35 km)	1938
Elara	7,301,100 miles	(11,750,000 km)	50 miles	(80 km)	1905
Ananke	12,990,000 miles	(20,900,000 km)	19 miles	(30 km)	1951
Carme	14,012,000 miles	(22,550,000 km)	25 miles	(40 km)	1938
Pasiphae	14,600,000 miles	(23,500,000 km)	31 miles	(50 km)	1908
Sinope	14,900,000 miles	(24,000,000 km)	22 miles	(35 km)	1914

million miles (24 million km) away. The table on the page 34 lists all the moons, their sizes, their distances from Jupiter, and when they were discovered.

Io: A Closer Look

Io is about the same size as Earth's Moon, but the two moons look very different. Photographs taken by *Voyager 1* showed us that Io has many active volcanoes. In fact, the space probe even took some images of a volcano erupting. The volcano was later named Pele, after the famous soccer player.

Io, the Galilean moon closest to Jupiter, has many active volcanoes.

Before this discovery, scientists thought Earth was the only planet in the solar system with active volcanoes. Today we know that Io is the most volcanically active body in the solar system. Its extensive volcanic activity is the result of internal heat caused by the gravitational pull of Jupiter and two of the planet's other moons.

In 1998, the *Galileo* spacecraft provided a close-up view of dozens of sulfur-spewing volcanoes on Jupiter's fiery moon Io. The probe also discovered that the lava spewing from the moon's volcanoes is sizzling hot. The lava erupting from a volcano called Pillan Patera was 3,140°F (1,730°C). According to Dr. Torrence Johnson, a Galileo project scientist at NASA's Jet Propulsion Laboratory, the volcanic activity we see on Io today may be very similar to ancient volcanic processes on Earth and the other planets.

Io's surface looks sort of like a pizza. It is covered with a fantastic patchwork of bright colors. Scientists think that the red, orange, yellow, and white spots may be sulfur deposits on top of the moon's volcanoes. For example, a volcano known as Masuri may look white because it is coated with frozen sulfur dioxide.

Images from the *Galileo* spacecraft show a volcano called Ru Patera giving off a 60-mile (97-km)-high blast of blue material. Scientists think the spray from the volcano may be a mixture of sulfur dioxide that consists partly of gas and partly of a frozen, snowlike material. Ru Patera's eruptions may have coated more than 15,000 square miles (38,800 sq. km) of Io's

surface with volcanic debris. Interestingly, Ru Patera seemed inactive when the Voyager spacecraft photographed it.

The surface of Earth's Moon is covered with **craters**—irregularly shaped holes created when an object hit it. Because asteroids, comets, and **meteorites** don't often crash into moons and planets, scientists think that objects with a lot of craters have older surfaces than objects with just a few craters.

Io does not appear to have craters, so many scientists suspect that Io's surface is relatively young. The planet's volcanic activity is probably causing the surface to change continuously.

This color-enhanced view of Io shows the volcano Ru Patera giving off a blast of blue material. The inset (upper left) shows the eruption in more detail.

Europa: A Closer Look

Europa is the smallest of the four Galilean moons. It is 1,942 miles (3,126 km) across. Europa, which is slightly smaller than Earth's Moon, is the sixth largest moon in the solar system.

Europa has a very smooth, bright surface. In fact, NASA scientists describe this moon as "the smoothest object in the solar system." Because there are only a few large craters on Europa, scientists believe its surface is relatively young—perhaps only about 30 million years old. That might sound pretty old to you, but remember that our Earth is about 4.6 billion years old.

The two types of terrain on Europa are clearly visible in this color-enhanced view of the moon.

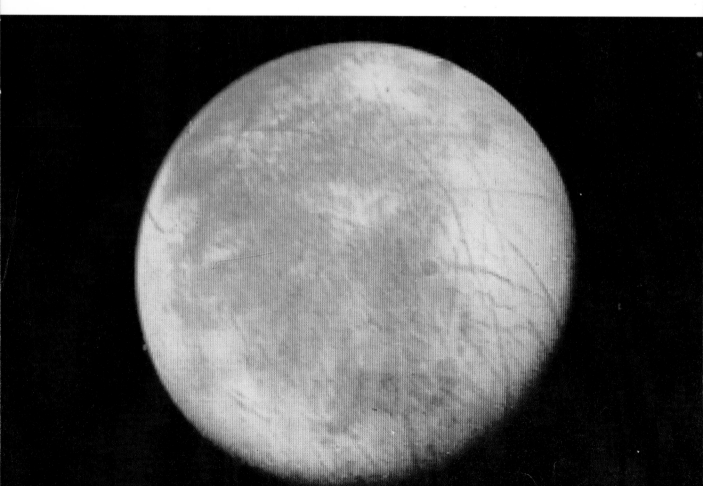

Europa's surface is covered with ice. Scientists believe this blanket of frozen water is more than 60 miles (97 km) thick in some places. Pictures taken by *Galileo* in 1997 showed scientists that Europa's icy crust contains two types of **terrain**. One type is brownish-gray and has many small hills. The second type looks a lot like the ice-covered Arctic Ocean on Earth. It consists of large, smooth plains with many cracks, grooves, and faults. Could an ocean of water or ice-and-water slush exist beneath Europa's icy surface? Some scientists think it may. Others aren't so sure that an ocean exists on Europa today, but they believe there may have been a large body of water on this moon millions of years ago.

They observed that large blocks of Europa's icy crust seem to move around. Perhaps these blocks are sliding over a watery layer, just as icebergs do on Earth. But how could liquid water

What Does "Europa" Mean

According to an ancient Greek legend, Europa was another young, beautiful girl that Zeus loved. When Zeus came to Europa in the form of a bull with wings, she climbed on the bull's back and they flew off to a beautiful Greek island.

exist on a moon with a surface temperature of −260°F (−162°C)? Scientists know that the gravitational fields of Jupiter and some of its moons cause Europa to bend as it orbits the king of the planets. This movement causes heat to build up deep inside Europa. Maybe all that heat could melt enough ice to form a liquid ocean beneath the moon's icy surface.

On Earth, some kinds of living creatures can exist in environments that are dark, have no oxygen, and are buried under thick layers of ice. Could the same be true on Europa? Scientists agree that the presence of water and heat suggests that life may have once existed on Europa.

The *Galileo* spacecraft also spotted brown stains on the moon's ice. Some scientists think these patches may be evidence of hydrogen cyanide and other chemicals necessary for life. According to NASA planetary scientist Richard Terrile, if these chemicals are mixed into the water, "That's a recipe for life."

Although Galileo's images suggest that an ocean may have once existed beneath Europa's crust, scientists do not know if an ocean is there today. And even though life could exist in such waters, there is no proof that it ever did. In the future, NASA may send an orbiter to Europa to perform tests that will determine whether an ocean ever existed there.

Ganymede: A Closer Look

Ganymede is Jupiter's largest moon, and it may be the largest moon in the entire solar system. It is bigger than the planets Mercury and Pluto. Because Ganymede is so large, it has enough gravity to hold onto a thin atmosphere. It also has its

Ganymede is Jupiter's largest moon.

own magnetic field. As far as scientists know, no other moon in our solar system has a magnetic field.

Ganymede has two different kinds of terrain. About 40 percent of its surface is covered by dark, heavily cratered regions. These areas are believed to be part of Ganymede's original surface. The rest of the moon, which scientists think is newer, is smoother, lighter in color, and has many grooves and ridges. Some of the grooves are thousands of miles long, and some of the ridges are 2,000 feet (700 m) high. At times, the ridges and grooves look as though they've been twisted.

Scientists think Ganymede has four distinct layers—a metal core; a rocky layer; a thick soft blanket of ice; and a thin, hard, icy crust. If they are correct, Ganymede's interior is very similar to Earth's.

Callisto: A Closer Look

Callisto is the third largest moon in the solar system—only Ganymede and Titan, a moon that orbits Saturn, are larger. Callisto is just a bit smaller than the planet Mercury. It has no atmosphere, but—like Europa—it may have an ocean of salty water beneath its icy crust. Scientists also think that Callisto has a small core.

Callisto is the most heavily cratered object in the solar system, so scientists think its surface is more than 4 billion years old. Callisto's craters appear as bright spots on its surface. Although Callisto's surface is darker than Jupiter's other moons, it is still twice as bright as Earth's Moon.

When scientists examined images taken by *Galileo*, they noticed seven distinct crater chains on Callisto. It's likely that these chains were formed when a comet broke into pieces and hit the moon.

Although landslides are gradually filling in some of Callisto's craters, there appears to be no volcanic activity or other important geologic processes on the moon. This is surprising. It is the largest object in the solar system that shows no sign of extensive resurfacing. As a result, some scientists describe Callisto as "a long-dead world."

What Does "Callisto" Mean

According to an ancient Greek legend, Callisto was a beautiful young girl who captured Zeus's attention. When Zeus's wife learned that he loved the girl, she turned Callisto into a bear. To protect Callisto from hunters, Zeus lifted her up to the heavens. There the girl sparkled among the stars as the Great Bear constellation. The brightest stars of the Great Bear form the Big Dipper.

Jupiter's Rings: A Closer Look

Scientists have known about Saturn's rings for more than 300 years, but it was *Voyager 1* that discovered the rings around Jupiter. Jupiter's rings are much more difficult to see because they are made of very small, dark particles of dust and rock. Unlike Saturn's rings, Jupiter's rings do not appear to contain any ice.

It is very difficult to create an accurate view of Jupiter's rings. Here we see the rings in yellow and the edge of the planet in green.

In 1998, *Galileo* provided information that allowed scientists to identify four separate rings. Data collected by the spacecraft also helped scientists figure out how the rings formed. Jupiter has four rings—an inner cloud-like ring called a halo; a large, flat main ring; and two very faint gossamer rings.

Each of the rings consists of dust hurled into space when meteorites strike one of Jupiter's small inner moons. The halo is made up of debris that was once part of Metis, Jupiter's innermost moon. Similarly, the main ring was formed from particles that were once part of the tiny moon Adrastea. The two gossamer rings are made up of material from Amalthea and Thebe. Scientists suspect that the faint rings that surround Neptune and Uranus are also created by dust from the planets' moons.

Amalthea may provide material for two of Jupiter's rings.

A group of excited scientists watch as fragments of the comet Shoemaker-Levy 9 crash into Jupiter.

Chapter Five

The Greatest Show in Space

From July 16 to 23, 1994, scientists and amateur stargazers around the world waited anxiously with their telescopes fixed on Jupiter. They were preparing to see a comet named Shoemaker-Levy 9 smash into Jupiter. This was the thrilling conclusion to a story that began more than a year earlier.

In March 1993, planetary scientists Eugene and Carolyn Shoemaker and David Levy identified a new comet near Jupiter. Like all comets, Shoemaker-Levy 9 originally orbited the Sun, but by the time it was discovered, the comet had already been caught in Jupiter's mighty gravitational field and broken apart. Shoemaker-Levy 9 was now orbiting the king of the planets as twenty-one large fragments and thousands of tiny pieces. Some scientists said these fragments reminded them of a "string of pearls" in space.

It didn't take long for scientists to realize that Shoemaker-Levy 9 would soon crash into Jupiter. Scientists had never seen an event like this before, but they warned people not to get their hopes up. They weren't sure what the impact would look like. Would there be a spectacular explosion or just a slight fizzle? Since the comet would hit just out of sight, on the side of Jupiter facing away from Earth, many scientists didn't expect anything too impressive. They were in for a big surprise!

As the first chunk of the comet hit, there was a huge explosion. This was the beginning of an incredible show that lasted for several days. The impacts were so powerful that they sent giant fountains of gas thousands of miles above Jupiter's atmosphere. Large, dark pieces of comet debris were hurled into space. Some of these chunks were large enough to be viewed by people using small telescopes set up in their backyards.

Scientists on Earth calculated that one of the fragments hit Jupiter with a force equal to 6 million nuclear bombs. Although the fragments landed on Jupiter's far side, they came into full view as the planet swiftly rotated. The Hubble Space Telescope, which orbits our planet, and *Galileo*, a spacecraft that traveled to Jupiter, sent photos of the spectacular event back to Earth.

Could a Comet Strike Earth?

After seeing the tremendous explosions on Jupiter, many people began to wonder what would happen if a comet hit Earth. Many scientists believe that such an impact wiped out the dinosaurs 65 million years ago.

Experts predict that if a comet or asteroid crashed into Earth, the dust and debris blown into our atmosphere would block out the Sun's rays. Our planet would then cool significantly, making it impossible for many living things to survive.

An artist's view of **Galileo** *launching from the Space* **Shuttle** Atlantis

Chapter Six

The Future

The *Galileo* spacecraft's exploration of Jupiter excited scientists tremendously. Each new look at the planet, its moons, and its rings revealed more interesting information about the king of the planets. Some scientists hope to study Europa and Jupiter even more closely in the future. They wonder whether Europa ever supported life. They also think that Jupiter may hold the key to solving many puzzling mysteries about Earth and the other planets in our solar system.

These scientists think all the planets, moons, asteroids, and comets formed from a giant cloud of material that

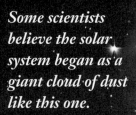

Some scientists believe the solar system began as a giant cloud of dust like this one.

orbited the Sun. The heavier materials stayed closer to the Sun, but lightweight materials, such as hydrogen and helium, were pushed to the outer regions of the solar system. Many of these materials were collected by Jupiter. As the planet grew larger and its gravitational pull grew stronger, Jupiter became better at holding on to the lightweight materials than other planets.

If these theories are correct, studying Jupiter could teach us a great deal about the early history of Earth and the other planets. Jupiter could also provide clues about how the solar system formed. Thus, future missions to the king of the planets may help us to better understand the past.

Glossary

asteroid—a large piece of rock that formed at the same time as the Sun and planets.

atmosphere—the various gases that surround a planet or other body in space.

axis—the imaginary line running from pole to pole through a planet's center. A planet spins, or rotates, along its axis.

belt—one of the darker bands of clouds in Jupiter's atmosphere.

comet—a small ball of rock and ice that orbits the Sun. When it gets close to the Sun, some of the ice melts and releases gases. These gases form a tail behind the comet.

core—the centermost region of a planet.

crater—an irregular oval-shaped hole created by a collision with another object.

density—an object's mass divided by its volume.

gravitational field—the area of space affected by a planet's gravity.

gravity—the force that pulls objects toward the center of a planet or other body in space.

magnetic field—the area surrounding a planet in which magnetic force is felt.

magnetosphere—the area of space around a planet that is affected by the planet's magnetic field.

mass—the amount of matter or material in an object.

meteorite—a particle of dust or rock that hits the surface of another object, such as a moon or planet.

orbit—the curved path followed by one body going around another body in space.

radiation belt—a region around Jupiter where the electrically charged particles that make up solar wind congregate. The particles are trapped by Jupiter's magnetic field.

solar system—the Sun and all the objects—planets, moons, asteroids, and comets—that orbit it.

solar wind—a stream of particles that are given off by the Sun.

space probe—an unmanned spacecraft carrying scientific instruments that orbits the Sun on its way to one or more planets. It may fly past a planet it has been aimed at, orbit the planet, or, in some cases, even land there.

terrain—the physical features of a piece of land.

volume—the total amount of space an object occupies.

zone—one of the lighter bands of clouds in Jupiter's atmosphere.

To Find Out More

Books

Berger, Melvin. *Where Are the Stars During the Day?* Nashville, TN: Ideals Children's Books, 1993.

Branley, Franklyn Mansfield. *The Sun and the Solar System.* New York: Twenty-First Century Books, 1996.

Heathcote, Nick. *The New Discovery Book of Space.* New York: New Discovery Books, 1994.

Kallen, Stuart A. *The Race to Space.* Edina, MN: Abdo & Daughters, 1996.

Levy, David. *Stars and Planets.* Alexandria, VA: Time-Life Books, 1996.

Lippincott, Kristen. *Astronomy*. New York: Dorling Kindersley, 1994.

Moore, Patrick. *Space Travel for Beginners*. New York: Press Syndicate of University of Cambridge, 1992.

Simon, Seymour. *Destination Jupiter*. New York: Morrow, 1998.

Sipiera, Paul. *The Solar System*. Danbury, CT: Children's Press, 1997.

Stoot, Carole. *Night Sky*. New York: Dorling Kindersley, 1993.

Verdet, Jean-Pierre. *Earth, Sky, and Beyond: A Journey Through Space*. New York: Lodestar, 1995.

Vogt, Gregory. *Jupiter*. Brookfield, CT: Millbrook, 1993.

Walker, Jane. *The Solar System*. Brookfield, CT: Millbrook, 1995.

Online Sites

The Jovian System
http://www.jpl.nasa.gov/galileo/Jovian.html#moons.
This site is maintained by NASA's Jet Propulsion Laboratory. It has information about and images of Jupiter and its moons.

Jupiter

http://seds.lpl.arizona.edu/nineplanets/nineplanets/jupiter.html

Provides an up-to-date general introduction to the planet Jupiter and includes links to images.

Mission Home

www.missonhome.org

Describes how equipment designed for the space program can be adapted for practical uses on Earth.

NASA's Quest Project

http://quest.arc.nasa.gov

A list and description of NASA-sponsored educational programs.

Places To Visit

These museums and science centers are great places to learn more about Jupiter and the solar system.

Hansen Planetarium
15 South State Street
Salt Lake City, UT 84111

Howell Observatory
1400 W. Mars Hill Rd.
Flagstaff, AZ 86001

Miami Museum of Science and Space Transit Planetarium
3280 South Miami Avenue
Miami, FL 33129

The Newark Museum and Dreyfus Planetarium
49 Washington Street
P.O. Box 540
Newark, NJ 07101-0540

Reuben H. Fleet Space Theater and Science Center
1875 El Prado Way
P.O. Box 33303
San Diego, CA 92163-3303

Schiele Museum of Natural History and Planetarium, Inc.
1500 East Garrison Blvd.
Gastonia, NC 28054

Space Center
Top of New Mexico Highway 2001
P.O. Box 533
Alamogordo, NM 88311-0533

Space Center Houston
1601 NASA Road One
Houston, TX 77058

A Note
on Sources

It is important to use as many sources as possible when writing a book about space. I began by reading other books written for young people on my topic. Next, I read standard reference works for general information.

Because scientists learn new information about the planets all the time, I read recent articles in *The New York Times*, *Newsweek*, and a variety of science magazines. I also spoke with scientists at NASA's Solar System Exploration Division and the McDonald Observatory in Austin, Texas. The Jet Propulsion Laboratory in Pasadena, California, provided me with facts and figures sent back to Earth by space probes. I am especially grateful to Jose Olivarez, Director of Astronomy at the Chabot Observatory and Science Center in Oakland, California, for checking the accuracy of the manuscript.

—*Elaine Landau*

Index

Numbers in *italics* indicate illustrations.

About the Author

Popular author Elaine Landau has a B.A. degree from New York University and a Master's degree in library and information science from Pratt Institute.

She has written more than 100 non-fiction books for young people. Although Ms. Landau often writes about science, she has particularly enjoyed writing about the planets. She was fascinated to learn about the major strides the space program has made during the last few years.

Elaine Landau lives in Miami, Florida, with her husband and son, Michael. The trio can often be spotted at the Miami Museum of Science and Space Transit Planetarium.